# THE UK COCKTAIL BOOK

Classic, Modern & Super-Amazing Cocktail Recipes For Every Day incl. Whisky, Gin, Vodka & More

**Magnus Dilligan**

ISBN - 9798361974016

# TABLE OF CONTENTS

**Conclusion**....................................................................107

**DISCLAIMER**..............................................................108

# INTRODUCTION

Have you always wanted to learn how to make expensive-looking and stylish cocktails but you were afraid the whole subject was too hard to learn?

Good news is coming your way - it's entirely possible to make delicious, professional cocktails in the comfort of your own home.

Impress your guests with vodka, gin, whiskey, rum, and even non-alcoholic cocktails and forget having to wait at the bar any longer.

There are some basic techniques to learn when it comes to cocktail making, or mixology as it is better known. However, these aren't too hard to learn and once you have the right equipment in place, you'll be able to quickly master the techniques that will allow you to mix and muddle your way to cocktail heaven.

The downside of cocktail making is that you need to have a stock of ingredients on hand in order to whip up a batch of your favourite drink. For the most part, this is quite easy, as vodka, rum, whiskey, etc, are all quite easy to find. The mixers are often the difficult part, but in most supermarkets you will find the ingredients you need. However much buying the ingredients costs you, it will never be as much as several rounds of cocktails in a high quality bar.

Whether you want to relax at home with a drink in hand, or you have an upcoming event you need to cater for, learning how to make your favourite cocktails is never a waste of time. Your guests will be suitably impressed and if you have children or non-drinkers in attendance, you can learn about non-alcoholic cocktails very easily too. These cocktails simply omit the alcohol but use the same mixing techniques.

Modern & Classic Cocktails For Every Occasion is going to teach you

the basics and then take you through 50 delicious and easy cocktail recipes to replicate for yourself. The only question is, which will you start with?

# MIXOLOGY BASICS

Mixology is the word for mixing cocktails. A mixologist is therefore the bar person you see in a high quality bar who specialises in mixing fantastic and delicious cocktails for you. However, despite how complicated the whole thing looks, mixology can be learnt at home too.

Of course, that doesn't mean you can jump straight into the art of cocktail making without any practice or knowledge. It's important that you take the time to read, learn, and build confidence. Consider this your new hobby, something to enjoy whilst also helping you to take on board a brand new skill!

First, you need to stock up on the basic equipment you need to do the mixing and shaking. Secondly, you need to buy the ingredients, such as the alcoholic beverages and the mixers, and then you need to learn how to prepare and make the cocktails like a budding pro. From there, it's all about practice making true perfection. It might take a little time to get it spot-on, but you will get there, and you'll enjoy it in the process.

Sounds complicated? Not really. Let's break it down and help you understand what you need in terms of equipment, ingredients, and of course, help you understand the basic techniques to start mixing and shaking those cocktails in no time at all!

## Equipment

You cannot make cocktails properly without specific equipment. You might be tempted to just use the utensils you have at home, but you won't get the same results and your final outcome will be substandard. If you're serious about making cocktails to thrill your

guests and enjoy yourself, you need to invest a little. The good news is that it doesn't have to cost a fortune.

You might be tempted to buy bargain basement equipment, but mixology is a true art form. You wouldn't catch an illustrator using a blunt pencil, so don't attempt to make cocktails with equipment which is substandard or less than able to do the job! Having said that, you can easily find mixology bundles which contain all the basic equipment you need mix cocktails without much effort. Simply shop around and look for quality and the equipment will last longer as a result. Online is the place to go for the best deals and because mixology is so in demand as a hobby these days, you won't struggle to find a good choice.

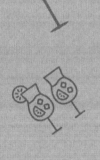

The basic tools you need are:

- **Jigger** - This is a tool which will help you to measure your ingredients and therefore create a high quality outcome. Jiggers come in all different shapes and sizes, but it's a good idea to purchase a variety pack so you have everything you need to hand. A cone-shaped jigger is the most common type you will find and usually measures 1.5oz of liquid.

- **Cocktail shaker** - The iconic cocktail tool! You'll find a few different shakers around, but the most common are the Cobbler and the Boston. It's a good idea to buy both but the Cobbler shaker is the best for beginners. You can move up to using the Boston as you become more au fait with how to make your favourite drinks. A Boston shaker has a pint glass on one side and a jug made of metal on the other side which covers the shaker and allows you to shake with ease, in a faster time. A cobbler is the simpler version you will have seen everywhere.

- **Strainer** - You will use a strainer for countless different cocktails so it's a good idea to invest in one from the start. A Cobbler cocktail shaker has a built-in strainer but the Boston version doesn't. Regardless, you won't use a strainer for every cocktail so you will need the individual tool handy. The most likely type you will find is called a Hawthorne striker and you place it on top of whatever glass you're serving your drink into and then pour the mixture on top. This then catches all the herbs and the pulp and gives you a smooth drink.

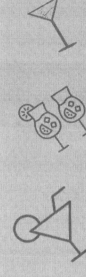

- **Muddler** - Muddlers are not commonly used but for cocktails such as mojitos, or others which require you to use herbs, you will need to muddle. This is a technique which allows you to get the scent and the taste out of any herbs you're using, without bruising the herb and creating a poor taste as a result.

- **Juicer** - Many cocktails call for fresh fruit juice and whilst you can use the varieties you purchase in a carton, they're just not as fresh tasting or as delicious as the juice from a fresh fruit! In order to get the juice out of the fruit you need a juicer. The good news is that this isn't a specialist piece of equipment and you can easily buy a juicer from a hardware store or even a supermarket!

- **Bar spoons** - These long handled spoons often have a spiral section on the handle and they are used to stir cocktails which don't require shaking. The spiral long handle helps you to mix tall glasses with ease, combining all ingredients completely. Many cocktails require careful stirring too, and the long-handled helps with that.

- **A variety of cocktail glasses** - Different cocktails are served in different glasses and if you want to present your creations in the best possible way, you'll need the right glasses for the job. The most common are a martini glass, a tumbler, a tall glass, and a champagne flute, but you'll find countless others beside! You don't have to go out and buy the whole range of cocktail glasses from the start, but you should do your research and buy the most common types you're going to use.

Finding cocktail mixing equipment isn't hard these days, thanks to the wonder of the Internet. You can easily search and find deals that won't cost the Earth and will allow you to mix delicious creations. The list above contains the basics you need to start mixing, but you will find that there are more in-depth equipment types as you become the expert mixologist in your own home. For now however, those can wait.

## Ingredients

Once you've got your tools, you need the ingredients to mix together and create cocktails. In this book, we're going to cover recipes which contain vodka, gin, whiskey and rum as the base ingredients, but you will find a few others you might need in addition, such as absinthe and Prosecco to name just two. It's best to stick to the recipe completely, otherwise you risk throwing off the subtle combination of flavours that makes the recipe so special.

Of course, most alcoholic spirits are easily accessible and you can purchase them when they're on offer, in order to save cash. It goes without saying that if you simply don't like whiskey, you just don't make the whiskey cocktails! Stick to your favourites and work on getting the taste perfect, rather than purchasing all the ingredients under the sun "just in case".

In addition to alcoholic beverages, you'll also need mixers and bitters. Again, these can be bought when they're on offer, but they're not particularly difficult to find. Most recipes call for the same types, so you're not going to waste money on anything too obscure. A very common ingredient however is fruit. Orange, lemon, lime, strawberry, raspberry, these are all very commonly used in cocktails, so you should stock up at the local market and enjoy as part of a healthy diet, as well as your cocktail making endeavours!

Of course, the last thing you're going to need a lot of is ice. Both ice cubes and crushed ice are very prevalent in cocktail making, so make sure you fill up your trays before you decide to make a batch of cocktails and you won't have a warm drink at the end.

If you can't find crushed ice in a store or you simply don't want to spend money on what is basically frozen water, all you need to do is place a few ice cubes in a sealable plastic bag and bash with the end of a rolling pin. Alternatively, you can place your ice cubes in the blender and blitz - voila! Free crushed ice!

## Preparation

When you're about to make a cocktail, it's a good idea to measure everything out beforehand. This makes the process far easier and less messy. Remember, cocktail making is an art and artists don't have bottles and remnants of fruit all over their counter whilst they're trying to create something wonderful!

The best advice is to look at the recipe and read it through to the end, making sure that you understand what you need to do. Then, identify the ingredients required and measure them out beforehand. After that, lay out the tools you need and start working through the recipe.

If your recipe calls for fresh juice, squeeze out the juice ahead of time and throw away the pieces you don't need. It's likely that if a recipe asks for fresh juice, it will also ask for slices or zest too, so don't forget to prepare those beforehand too and place them to one side.

Prepare the glasses required and keep them to one side too. Then, you're good to start!

## Techniques

There are various techniques you will need to master in order to create the best cocktails around. Practice truly does make perfect here, so don't worry if the first batch you make doesn't quite turn out to be as fantastic as you would like! You can practice in an empty glass or with fruit juice, to avoid wasting expensive ingredients beforehand.

Let's look at some of the basic techniques you'll be using in our recipes to come.

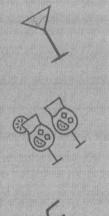

### Shaking

This is not simply a case of pouring everything into your cocktail shaker, putting the lid on and then shaking vigorously! If you shake too hard, you risk ruining the subtle flavours. Many cocktail recipes require shaking to combine liquids completely but as you start to make cream-based recipes or anything which contains eggs, you'll also need to shake. You'll also notice that most recipes that require the addition of fresh fruit juice are also shaken.

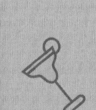

When shaking, you add ice into the shaker and continue to shake until the outside of the metal starts to feel cold. That means everything is combined, including the ice. Hold the shaker in both hands to avoid dropping it and making a real mess. Place one hand on the top of the shaker to hold the top in place and hold the base with the other hand to steady your shaking. Then, shake in a sharp manner, until the outside feels cold. This should only take a minute at the most.

### Straining

Another very common technique is straining. This means that you're getting rid of any pulps, seeds, herbs, or anything else that may cause your cocktail to be grainy or 'bitty'. You will use your Hawthorne strainer for this and simply place it over the top of your serving glass. The carefully pour the contents of your shaker or your jug into the strainer and allow the pure liquid to cascade into the serving glass below. You can then throw away the contents of the strainer.

Never attempt to strain a drink that contains crushed ice as it will simply clog up the inner workings and cause your efforts to stall. However, most strained recipes require ice cubes anyway.

## Muddling

Muddling is a less common technique but if you want to be an expert mixologist, it's one you need to learn. Mudding is used when you have herbs or fruit contained within a cocktail and the subtle flavours need to be released. For instance, you would muddle with a mojito, because of the mint.

Muddling needs to be done slowly and carefully, to avoid brushing the herb or the fruit. When this happens, the taste can be ruined.

Simply take your muddler and gently press down on the herb, e.g. the mint leaf. Some bar spoons contains a muddler on the back, so it's a 2 in 1 tool you can use. Some muddlers also look a little like a regular pestle you would use in cooking.

## Stirring

Along with shaking, stirring is another very common technique to learn. You will need a specialist bar spoon for this, so don't be tempted to use a regular spoon! Bar spoons have long, twisted handles which allow them to reach the bottom of the tallest glass and combine all ingredients to ensure the flavours are mixed.

Hold the glass in one hand and the bar spoon in the other and stir in a slow, circular motion. This is not like stirring a cup or tea or coffee, you need to move in a delicate motion to combine well.

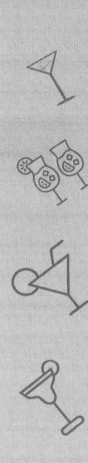

These are the basic techniques you need to use in order to create delicious cocktails from scratch. Of course, the most expert mixologists out there can do two things at once and they also use other in-depth techniques, such as flaming or building, but these aren't things you need to know about right now. You can easily create some of the best cocktails around by using these basic techniques alone.

Now it's time to get practical! In the coming chapters you will find recipes that contain some of the most common alcoholic ingredients, followed by a chapter which allows you to create non-alcoholic cocktails too. Either work your way through them all, or choose the ones which you think you're going to enjoy the most.

Remember, practice makes perfect, so don't give up if your first attempt isn't the best. With time, you'll be mixing up amazing cocktails with ease, and impressing your visitors in the process!

# VODKA COCKTAIL RECIPES

You can make an array of delicious recipes with a staple of vodka. To make vanilla vodka, one of the most common ingredients in most recipes, you simply add a little vanilla essence to your vodka, according to your taste.

Most other ingredients are readily available, such as fruits and sugar syrup.

Which one will you try first?

# MARTINI WITH A PASSIONFRUIT TWIST

*Time 5 minutes, serves 2*
*Net carbs: 16g/0.56oz, Fiber: 2g/0.07oz, Fat: 0g/0oz,*
*Protein: 1g/0.03oz, Kcal: 224*

## INGREDIENTS:

- 60ml vanilla flavoured vodka
- 1 tbsp fresh lime juice
- 1 tbsp sugar syrup
- 30ml quality passoa
- 2 passion fruits, cut into halves
- Prosecco for serving
- Handful of ice cubes

## PREPARATION:

| 1. | Prepare the passion fruit by removing the seeds and the skin, keeping the seeds to one side |

| 2. | Take a cocktail shaker and add the seeds |

| 3. | Add the passoa, vodka, sugar syrup, and the lime juice |

| 4. | Add a few ice cubes |

**5.** Give the shaker a good shake

**6.** Use a strainer to pour the drink into two martini-style glasses

**7.** Add a little Prosecco to the top

**8.** Add half a passion fruit to each glass

# CLASSIC SEX ON THE BEACH

*Time 5 minutes, serves 2*
*Net carbs: 8g/0.28oz, Fiber: 0.01g/0.003oz, Fat: 0g/0oz,*
*Protein: 1g/0.03oz, Kcal: 92*

## INGREDIENTS:

- 25ml schnapps, peach works best
- 50ml vodka
- 50ml fresh cranberry juice
- The juice of 2 oranges
- A handful of ice cubes

## PREPARATION:

| 1. | Take two tall cocktail glasses and add the ice to each |
| 2. | Take a large jug and add the schnapps, vodka and the cranberry and orange juices |
| 3. | Stir everything together well |
| 4. | Pour the cocktail into the glasses equally and stir carefully |
| 5. | Add a few slices from the orange for decoration |

# LONG ISLAND ICED TEA

*Time 5 minutes, serves 4*
*Net carbs: 16g/0.56oz, Fiber: 0g/0oz, Fat: 0g/0oz,*
*Protein: 0g/0oz, Kcal: 212*

## INGREDIENTS:

- ◆ 50ml gin
- ◆ 50ml vanilla flavoured vodka
- ◆ 50ml tequila
- ◆ 50ml rum
- ◆ 50ml triple sec
- ◆ A handful of ice cubes
- ◆ 100ml lime juice
- ◆ 500ml cola
- ◆ Lime wedges for decoration

## PREPARATION:

| 1. | Take a large jug and add the alcoholic beverages |

| 2. | Add the lime juice and top up to halfway with ice cubes |

3. Stir well - the outside of the jug should feel cold before you stop stirring

4. Pour in the cola and stir

5. Add the wedges of lime

6. Divide the cocktail between 4 tall glasses, pouring over more ice

# TRADITIONAL BLOODY MARY

*Time 5 minutes, serves 2*
*Net carbs: 8g/0.28oz, Fiber: 2g/0.07oz, Fat: 0g/0oz,*
*Protein: 2g/0.07oz, Kcal: 160*

## INGREDIENTS:

- 100ml vodka
- A handful of ice cubes
- 500ml tomato juice
- Tabasco sauce to taste
- Worcestershire sauce to taste
- 1tbsp fresh lemon juice
- A little black pepper to taste
- 2 sticks of celery for decoration

## PREPARATION:

| 1. | Take a large jug and add the ice |

| 2. | Next, add the tomato juice, lemon juice and the vodka |

| 3. | Add the two sauces according to your taste and a little pepper |

| | |
|---|---|
| **4.** | Give everything a stir until the outer side of the jug is cold |

| | |
|---|---|
| **5.** | Use a strainer to pour into 2 tall cocktail glasses |

| | |
|---|---|
| **6.** | Add a little ice to each and a stick of celery for decoration |

# JAMES BOND'S FAVOURITE MARTINI

*Time 5 minutes, serves 1*
*Net carbs: 0.01g/oz, Fiber: 0g/0oz, Fat: 0g/0oz,*
*Protein: 0g/0oz, Kcal: 174*

## INGREDIENTS:

- 1 tbsp vermouth, the dry version is best for this cocktail

- 60ml vodka

- The peel of a lemon for decoration

## PREPARATION:

|  |  |
|---|---|
| **1.** | Take a jug and combine the vermouth and vodka with some ice |

|  |  |
|---|---|
| **2.** | Pour into a cocktail shaker and give it a few good shakes |

|  |  |
|---|---|
| **3.** | Use a strainer to pour the cocktail into a martini glass |

|  |  |
|---|---|
| **4.** | Decorate with the lemon peel |

# THE SUNSET OVER WATERLOO

*Time 10 minutes, serves 8*
*Net carbs: 8g/0.28oz, Fiber: 0g/0oz, Fat: 0g/0oz,*
*Protein: 0g/0oz, Kcal: 124*

## INGREDIENTS:

- 100ml schnapps, peach works best for this cocktail
- 200ml vanilla flavoured vodka
- A little grenadine to taste
- 500ml peach juice, chilled
- A little lemonade
- A handful of fresh or frozen raspberries
- A handful of ice cubes

## PREPARATION:

1. Take a mixing jug and add the vodka, juice, and schnapps, combining well

2. Pour the cocktail evenly between 8 glasses

3. Add a few ice cubes to each glass and fill up to the top with lemonade

**4.** Take a teaspoon and pour a little of the grenadine over the spoon, into the glass

**5.** Decorate with the raspberries

# APPLE & GINGER VODKA PUNCH

*Time 5 minutes, serves 10*
*Net carbs: 20g/0.70oz, Fiber: 0g/0oz, Fat: 0g/0oz,*
*Protein: 0g/0oz, Kcal: 198*

## INGREDIENTS:

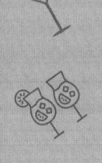

- 500ml apple juice

- 500ml vanilla flavoured vodka

- 1 litre ginger beer

- The juice of 2 limes

- 2 limes sliced into wedges

- 1 thinly sliced apple

- A small piece of peeled and sliced ginger

## PREPARATION:

1. Take a large jug and add all the liquid ingredients, combining well

2. Add the ginger, wedges of lime, and the apple to the jug and mix once more

3. Add ice to your glasses and pour the cocktail over the ice

# CHOCOLATE ORANGE VODKA

*Time 25 minutes, serves 4*
*Net carbs: 19g/0.67oz, Fiber: 1g/0.03oz, Fat: 4g/0.14oz,*
*Protein: 1g/0.03oz, Kcal: 232*

## INGREDIENTS:

- 100ml vodka
- 100ml creme de cacao
- 60ml orange liqueur
- 40ml fresh orange juice
- 100g caster sugar
- The zest of 1 large orange
- 100ml cold water
- A handful of ice cubes
- A little dark chocolate, grated, for decoration

## PREPARATION:

1. Take a small saucepan and combine the water with the sugar and orange zest. Allow to boil, stirring regularly

2. Allow the syrup to cool and strain into a small bowl

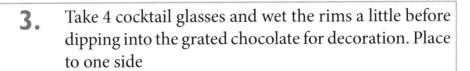

3.     Take 4 cocktail glasses and wet the rims a little before dipping into the grated chocolate for decoration. Place to one side

4.     Take a cocktail shaker and add the creme de cacao, vodka, orange juice, and the stained syrup you just made

5.     Add the ice and shake

6.     Pour into the prepared glasses

# FLORAL PROSECCO & VODKA COCKTAIL

*Time 15 minutes, serves 4*
*Net carbs: 9g/0.31oz, Fiber: 0g/0oz, Fat: 0g/0oz,*
*Protein: 0g/0oz, Kcal: 136*

## INGREDIENTS:

♦ 100ml vodka

♦ 300ml Prosecco

♦ 25ml ginger beer or cordial

♦ The juice of 1 orange

♦ The juice of 1 lemon

♦ A few hibiscus flower, including the syrup

♦ A handful of ice cubes

## PREPARATION:

1. Take a cocktail shaker and combine the lemon juice, orange juice, vodka, and ginger, with a little ice

2. Take 4 champagne glasses and add a hibiscus flower inside each one

3. Use a strainer to pour the cocktail into each glass, leaving space for the Prosecco

**4.** Add a little Prosecco to each glass

**5.** Top with a teaspoon of the hibiscus syrup

# CITRUS & APEROL PUNCH

*Time 5 minutes, serves 4*
*Net carbs: 7g/0.24oz, Fiber: 0g/0oz, Fat: 0g/0oz,*
*Protein: 0g/0oz, Kcal: 264*

## INGREDIENTS:

- 100ml limoncello

- 100ml vodka

- 200ml Aperol

- 300ml fresh orange juice

- 1 tbsp triple sec

- Orange slices for decoration

## PREPARATION:

| 1. | Take a mixing jug and combine all the ingredients, apart from the orange slices |

| 2. | Take 4 glasses and add ice to each |

| 3. | Pour the cocktail into each glass |

| 4. | Decorate with orange slices |

# CREAMY WHITE RUSSIAN

*Time 5 minutes, serves 1*
*Net carbs: 9.7g/oz, Fiber: 0g/0oz, Fat: 2.9g/oz,*
*Protein: 0.5g/oz, Kcal: 246*

## INGREDIENTS:

- 2 tbsp Kahlua

- 60ml vodka

- 1 tbsp double cream

- Handful of ice cubes

## PREPARATION:

| 1. | Take a mixing jug and combine the Kahlua, vodka and cream carefully |

| 2. | Place a few ice cubes in a tumbler glass |

| 3. | Pour the cocktail and enjoy whilst cold |

# GIN COCKTAIL RECIPES

Gin is the drink of the moment, without a doubt! There are countless new flavours of gin you can try on the market, but if you want to create a good, old fashioned cocktail with this delicious spirit, there are plenty to try.

When mixing cocktails with gin, unless the recipe calls for it, always use plain gin, rather than pink or any other flavour. The subtle flavours of the cocktail will be knocked out of kilter if you use a strong flavoured beverage.

Be prepared to be amazed!

# FIZZY GIN

*Time 5 minutes, serves 1*
*Net carbs: 5g/0.17oz, Fiber: 0g/0oz, Fat: 0g/0oz,*
*Protein: 0.1g/0.003oz, Kcal: 155*

## INGREDIENTS:

- 25ml fresh lemon juice
- 50ml gin
- 2 tsp sugar syrup
- A little sparkling water
- A handful of ice cubes
- A slice of lemon to decorate

## PREPARATION:

| 1. | Take a cocktail shaker and add all the ingredients, except for the lemon slices |
| 2. | Fill the shaker up with the ice cubes |
| 3. | Shake until the outside feels frosty |
| 4. | Use a strainer to pour the cocktail into the glass |
| 5. | Add a bit more ice and decorate with the lemon slices |

# RED BERRY GIN

*Time 15 minutes, serves 10*
*Net carbs: 3g/0.10oz, Fiber: 0g/0oz, Fat: 0g/0oz,*
*Protein: 0g/0oz, Kcal: 67*

## INGREDIENTS:

- 400g of sliced strawberries. You can use raspberries if you prefer
- 100g caster sugar
- 700ml gin

## PREPARATION:

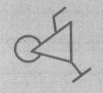

1. Take a large mixing bowl and add the berries and sugar, combining well

2. Add the gin and combine once more

3. Pour the mixing into a sterilised jar and seal

4. Keep the jar in the refrigerator and give it a quick stir every couple of days, for no longer than three weeks' duration

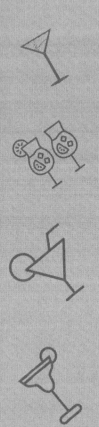

| **5.** | Once ready to serve, use a strainer to pour the cocktail |
|---|---|

| **6.** | Serve with ice cubes |
|---|---|

# CLASSIC TOM COLLINS

*Time 12 minutes, serves 1*
*Net carbs: 17g/0.59oz, Fiber: 0g/0oz, Fat: 0g/0oz,*
*Protein: 0g/0oz, Kcal: 92*

## INGREDIENTS:

- ◆ 25ml fresh lemon juice

- ◆ 125ml soda water

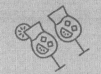

- ◆ 25ml sugar syrup

- ◆ 50ml gin

- ◆ A handful of ice cubes

- ◆ A few slices of lemon for decoration

## PREPARATION:

| 1. | Take a mixing jug and add all the liquid ingredients, combining well |

| 2. | Take a Collins glass and add a handful of ice cubes |

| 3. | Pour the cocktail into the glass and decorate with a lemon slice |

# TRADITIONAL NEGRONI COCKTAIL

*Time 5 minutes, serves 1*
*Net carbs: 4g/0.14oz, Fiber: 0g/0oz, Fat: 0g/0oz,*
*Protein: 0g/0oz, Kcal: 131*

## INGREDIENTS:

- 25ml vermouth, the sweet version works well with this cocktail

- 25ml Campari

- 25ml gin

- A handful of ice cubes

- A few orange slices for decoration

## PREPARATION:

1. Take a mixing jug and add the Campari, gin, and vermouth, combining well

2. Add the ice and stir until the outside of the container starts to feel icy

3. Use a strainer to pour the drink into a tumbler glass

4. Add some more ice and garnish with orange slices

# SLOE GIN

*Time 15 minutes, serves 1*
*Net carbs: 13g/0.45oz, Fiber: 0.4g/0.01oz, Fat: 0g/0oz,*
*Protein: 0.2g/0.007oz, Kcal: 198*

## INGREDIENTS:

- 25ml fresh lemon juice
- 25ml gin
- 50ml sloe gin
- A handful of ice cubes
- 100ml water
- Crushed ice
- 1 tbsp juniper berries
- 100g caster sugar

## PREPARATION:

| 1. | Take a small saucepan and add the sugar and water, with the juniper berries |

| 2. | Bring the pan to the boil and stir regular |

3. Once boiling, remove the pan from the heat and use a fork to mash the berries down until they're completely liquid. You may find it easier to use a potato masher in some cases

4. Place the pan to one side to cool

5. If you are storing the syrup for later, use a strainer to pour into a sterilised jar. You can keep this refrigerator for two weeks

6. Take a cocktail shaker and add the two types of gin, the lemon juice and add 2 teaspoons of the juniper syrup

7. Add a few ice cubes and shake until the outside of the shaker is cold

8. Add some crushed ice to a tumbler

9. Use a strainer to pour into the glass

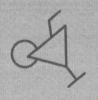

# REFRESHING SUMMER G&T

*Time 5 minutes, serves 1*
*Net carbs: 9g/0.31oz, Fiber: 0g/0oz, Fat: 0g/0oz,*
*Protein: 0g/0oz, Kcal: 101*

## INGREDIENTS:

♦ 2 tbsp gin

♦ A large cucumber, cut into long slices

♦ A handful of coriander

♦ A little tonic water to serve

♦ A handful of ice cubes

## PREPARATION:

| 1. | Take a tumbler glass and add a few ice cubes |
|---|---|

| 2. | Add the gin and a few sprigs of the coriander |
|---|---|

| 3. | Place a slice of cucumber into the glass to act as a stirrer but also for taste |
|---|---|

| 4. | Top up with the glass with your desired amount of tonic water |
|---|---|

| 5. | Combine carefully |
|---|---|

# CLASSIC G&T WITH A SPICY KICK

*Time 5 minutes, serves 1*
*Net carbs: 6g/0.21oz, Fiber: 0g/0oz, Fat: 0g/0oz,*
*Protein: 0.003g/oz, Kcal: 158*

## INGREDIENTS:

- ◆ 100ml tonic water
- ◆ 50ml cardamom gin
- ◆ 3 cardamom pods
- ◆ A handful of ice cubes

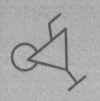

## PREPARATION:

| 1. | Take a large glass and add the ice |
|---|---|

| 2. | Pour the cardamom gin into the glass |
|---|---|

| 3. | Take the cardamom pods and crush until they open |
|---|---|

| 4. | Add the pods to the glass |
|---|---|

| 5. | Add the tonic water and combine |
|---|---|

| 6. | Add more ice if you prefer |
|---|---|

# RHUBARB FLAVOURED GIN

*Time 10 minutes, serves 10*
*Net carbs: 7g/0.24oz, Fiber: 0g/0oz, Fat: 0g/0oz,*
*Protein: 0g/0oz, Kcal: 63*

## INGREDIENTS:

- 400g caster sugar
- 800ml gin
- 1kg stalks of rhubarb

## PREPARATION:

1. Give the rhubarb a wash and cut away the leaves and the base, to leave the stalks

2. Cut into lengths of around 3cm

3. Take a large glass jar and add the sugar

4. Place the rhubarb into the jar and shake to coat and combine

5. Seal the jar and leave to one side overnight

6. Add the gin to the jar and shake everything to combine once more

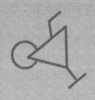

7. If you are storing the gin, it will keep for around 4 weeks

8. Once you're ready to serve, take a large glass and add some ice

9. User a strainer to pour the drink into the glass

# THE ICONIC SINGAPORE SLING

*Time 5 minutes, serves 1*
*Net carbs: 19g/0.67oz, Fiber: 0g/0oz, Fat: 0.1g/0.003oz,*
*Protein: 0.2g/0.007oz, Kcal: 233*

## INGREDIENTS:

- 25ml cherry brandy
- 25ml gin
- 25ml Benedictine
- Angostura bitters to taste

- 25ml fresh lime juice
- 50ml fresh pineapple juice
- Sparkling water to taste

- A handful of ice cubes
- Glace cherries to decorate

## PREPARATION:

1. Take a large jug and add the brandy, Benedictine, and the gin, combining well

2. Add the ice and the bitters and combine once more

3. Stir until the outer edge of the glass feels icy

4. Take a tall cocktail glass and add the lime and pineapple juices

5. Add the alcohol mixture and stir carefully

6. Top the glass up with the sparkling water

7. Add the cherry as a garnish

# FESTIVE FRUITY GIN

*Time 5 minutes, serves 4*
*Net carbs: 12g/0.42oz, Fiber: 0g/0oz, Fat: 0g/0oz,*
*Protein: 0.003g/0oz, Kcal: 115*

## INGREDIENTS:

- 100ml gin
- Half a sliced lemon
- 4 cloves
- 4 bay leaves
- 2 crushed cardamom pods
- 400ml fresh apple juice
- 1 cinnamon stick
- 0.5 tsp coriander seeds
- 1 tsp honey, the runny version works best
- 3 crushed juniper berries

## PREPARATION:

| 1. | Take four heatproof glasses |
|---|---|

| 2. | Divide the 100ml of gin between the four glasses equally |
|---|---|

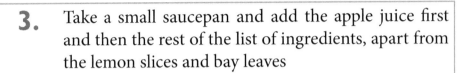

**3.** Take a small saucepan and add the apple juice first and then the rest of the list of ingredients, apart from the lemon slices and bay leaves

**4.** Over a low heat, allow the mixture to simmer

**5.** Remove from the heat and take a mixing jug

**6.** Use a strainer to pour the mixture into the jug

**7.** Divide the mixture between the glasses equally

**8.** Combine with a spoon carefully

**9.** Decorate with a bay leaf in each glass and a slice of lemon

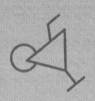

# WHISKEY COCKTAIL RECIPES

Whilst there aren't as many whiskey cocktails as there are for some other spirits, these are some of the most decadent and expensive you will come across. If you want to seriously impress your guests, perhaps as a nightcap after a delicious homemade meal, choose one of the recipes below.

Most recipes call for bourbon or rye whiskey, but it's really whatever you prefer to your own taste.

Be warned, these cocktails are quite strong!

# WARMING WHISKEY SOUR

*Time 10 minutes, serves 2*
*Net carbs: 3g/0.10oz, Fiber: 0g/0oz, Fat: 0g/0oz,*
*Protein: 0g/0oz, Kcal: 76*

## INGREDIENTS:

- ◆ 50ml bourbon
- ◆ 1 tbsp lemon juice, fresh is best
- ◆ 1 tbsp orange juice, fresh is best
- ◆ 0.5 tbsp sugar syrup
- ◆ Orange slices
- ◆ Crushed ice
- ◆ A little honey for decoration

## PREPARATION:

| 1. | Take two whiskey tumblers and add a little honey to the rim of each glass |
|---|---|

| 2. | Add the crushed ice equally to each glass |
|---|---|

| 3. | Take a cocktail shaker and add the bourbon and the orange, lemon, and sugar syrups |
|---|---|

| 4. | Shake to combine |
|---|---|

**5.** Use a strainer to pour the cocktail equally into each glass

**6.** Decorate the glass with a slice of orange

# CLASSIC SAZERAC

*Time 10 minutes, serves 4*
*Net carbs: 8g/0.28oz, Fiber: 0g/0oz, Fat: 0g/0oz,*
*Protein: 0g/0oz, Kcal: 168*

## INGREDIENTS:

- 50ml sugar syrup
- 1 tsp Peychaud's bitters
- 0.5 tsp Angostura bitters
- 200ml whiskey, the rye variety works well with this cocktail

- 2 tsp absinthe
- 25ml cold water
- A handful of ice cubes
- A little orange zest to decorate

## PREPARATION:

| 1. | Take four whiskey tumblers and add the absinthe to just one glass, swirling around the bottom of the glass |

| 2. | Pour the absinthe into the next glass and repeat, covering all four glasses |

**3.** Take a large mixing jug and add the bitters, the whiskey, and the sugar syrup. Add the water and ice cubes. Combine until he outside of the jug feels icy

**4.** Use a strainer to pour the cocktail into each glass equally

**5.** Take a piece of orange zest and twist it over one glass, dropping it inside. Repeat with all four glasses

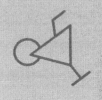

# REFRESHING MINT JULEP

*Time 5 minutes, serves 1*
*Net carbs: 9g/0.31oz, Fiber: 0g/0oz, Fat: 0g/0oz,*
*Protein: 0g/0oz, Kcal: 187*

## INGREDIENTS:

- 65ml bourbon
- 12.5ml sugar syrup
- 10 fresh mint leaves
- A handful of ice cubes
- Crushed ice

## PREPARATION:

1. Take a cocktail shaker and add the bourbon, sugar syrup, and the mint. Add the ice cubes and shake well

2. Fill a julep glass or a highball glass with crushed ice

3. Use a strainer to pour the cocktail into the glass

4. Use a long-handled spoon and churn the cocktail by moving it around quickly inside the glass

5. Add a little more crushed ice and serve with a straw

# TRADITIONAL WHISKEY MIX

*Time 5 minutes, serves 1*
*Net carbs: 7.2g/0.25oz, Fiber: 0.2g/0.007oz, Fat: 0g/0oz,*
*Protein: 0.2g/0.007oz, Kcal: 191*

## INGREDIENTS:

- ♦ 60ml bourbon

- ♦ 2 dashes of Angostura bitters

- ♦ 2 tsp sugar syrup

- ♦ A little soda water

- ♦ A slice of orange for decoration

- ♦ A dash of cold water

- ♦ A handful of ice cubes

## PREPARATION:

**1.** Take a small tumbler and add the sugar syrup, bitters and the cold water

**2.** Stir carefully until everything is combined

**3.** Add the ice cubes to the glass and pour the whiskey over the top

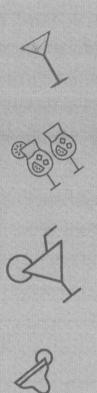

**4.** Add the soda water and mix carefully

**5.** Add a slice of orange for decoration

# CLASSIC HOT TODDY

*Time 5 minutes, serves 2*
*Net carbs: 10g/0.35oz, Fiber: 1g/0.03oz, Fat: 0.1g/0.03oz,*
*Protein: 0.3g/0.01oz, Kcal: 108*

## INGREDIENTS:

- 3 tsp honey, runny honey works best with this cocktail
- 50ml whiskey
- The juice of one lemon
- A few lemon slices for decoration
- 2 cloves
- 200ml boiling water
- 1 halved stick of cinnamon

## PREPARATION:

| 1. | Take a small mixing jug and combine the honey and the whiskey |
|----|----|
| 2. | Take two glasses, heatproof, and add a cinnamon stick half to each |
| 3. | Add 100ml of boiling water to each glass |
| 4. | Divide the lemon juice between the glasses |

**5.** Decorate each glass with lemon slices and one clove in each

**6.** Serve whilst still hot

# SOUR, NEW YORK STYLE

*Time 10 minutes, serves 1*
*Net carbs: 11g/0.38oz, Fiber: 0g/0oz, Fat: 0g/0oz,*
*Protein: 2g/0.07oz, Kcal: 191*

## INGREDIENTS:

- 50ml whiskey, rye whiskey works best with this cocktail

- 2 tsp maple syrup

- 25ml fresh lemon juice

- A dash of bitter orange

- 20ml red wine

- 1 tbsp egg white

- A handful of ice cubes

## PREPARATION:

| 1. | Take a cocktail shaker and add the whiskey, maple syrup, orange bitters, and lemon juice |

| 2. | Place the egg white onto a small plate and stir quickly with a spoon to loosen up |

| 3. | Pour the egg white into the shaker and shake |

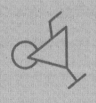

**4.** Add some ice cubes and shake once more, until the outside feels cold

**5.** Take your serving glass and strain the mixture inside, leaving a little space at the top

**6.** Fill up the rest of the glass with the red wine

**7.** After a couple of seconds, the wine will float to just underneath where the frothy section is (the egg white)

# MANHATTAN WHISKEY

*Time 5 minutes, serves 1*
*Net carbs: 3g/0.10oz, Fiber: 0g/0oz, Fat: 0g/0oz,*
*Protein: 0g/0oz, Kcal: 163*

## INGREDIENTS:

- 50ml bourbon

- 25ml vermouth (rosso is best)

- 2 dashes of Angostura bitters

- A handful of ice cubes

- 5ml cherry syrup (from a jar of maraschino cherries)

- 1 maraschino cherry for decoration

- A twist of lemon for decoration

## PREPARATION:

1. Take a mixing jug and add all the ingredients, apart from the decorations

2. Combine gently with a bar spoon

3. Use a strainer to pour into your serving glass

4. Add the cherry and twist of lemon on top for decoration

# CREAMY BOURBON

*Time 5 minutes, serves 2*
*Net carbs: 6g/0.21oz, Fiber: 0g/0oz, Fat: 2g/0.07oz,*
*Protein: 1g/0.03oz, Kcal: 95*

## INGREDIENTS:

- ◆ 4 tbsp creme de cacao
- ◆ 4 tbsp fresh lemon juice
- ◆ 4 tbsp bourbon
- ◆ 4 tsp caster sugar
- ◆ A handful of ice cubes
- ◆ A little orange zest for decoration

## PREPARATION:

| 1. | Take a cocktail shaker and combine all the ingredients |
|---|---|
| 2. | Shake to combine, until the outside of the shaker is cold |
| 3. | Take two martini glasses and pour the cocktail inside |
| 4. | Decorate with zest and serve |

# TRADITIONAL IRISH WHISKEY

*Time 5 minutes, serves 1*
*Net carbs: 14g/0.49oz, Fiber: 0g/0oz, Fat: 0g/0oz,*
*Protein: 0g/0oz, Kcal: 104*

## INGREDIENTS:

- 10ml Sauternes
- 40ml Irish whiskey
- 10ml elderflower (cordial)
- A handful of ice cubes
- A little lemon zest for decoration

## PREPARATION:

| 1. | Add the ingredients to a mixing jug |
|---|---|

| 2. | Use a bar spoon to carefully coming everything together |
|---|---|

| 3. | Make sure the ice cubes have melted slightly before serving |
|---|---|

| 4. | Pour into your cocktail glass |
|---|---|

| 5. | Garnish with a little lemon zest for decoration |
|---|---|

# RUM COCKTAIL RECIPES

With the tase of the tropics, rum has been a firm favourite for many years and is one of the baseline ingredients in many a popular cocktail. The famous mojito is just one you can try to make in your own home, and if you want to recreate the feel of the Caribbean on a warm summer's day, a rum-based punch will do the trick.

There are many different types of rum on the market, but as with gin, it's best to stick to the regular variety when making cocktails, unless specified in the recipe.

Mojito, punch, or something else - which will it be?

# CARIBBEAN RUM PUNCH

*Time 5 minutes, serves 2*
*Net carbs: 23g/0.81oz, Fiber: 0g/0oz, Fat: 0g/0oz,*
*Protein: 1g/0.03oz, Kcal: 271*

## INGREDIENTS:

- 150ml rum, golden rum works well with this cocktail
- 50ml sugar syrup
- 175ml fresh orange juice
- 75ml fresh lime juice
- A little grated nutmeg
- A little grenadine syrup
- A little Angostura bitters
- A handful of ice cubes
- A few orange slices for decoration
- 2 maraschino cherries for decoration

## PREPARATION:

1. Take a large mixing jug and add the orange and lime juices, sugar syrup, Angostura bitters, grenadine and rum, stirring to combine

2. Place the jug in the refrigerator for one hour

**3.** Take two cocktail glasses and divide the drink between them evenly

**4.** Sprinkle a little nutmeg over the top of each glass

**5.** Add an orange slice and a cherry to each glass as decoration

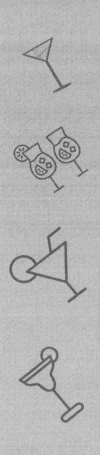

# THE ICONIC PINA COLADA

*Time 5 minutes, serves 1*
*Net carbs: 14.3g/0.50oz, Fiber: 0.5g/0.02oz, Fat: 12.7g/0.44oz,*
*Protein: 1.1g/0.03oz, Kcal: 314*

## INGREDIENTS:

- ◆ 60ml white rum
- ◆ 120ml fresh pineapple juice
- ◆ 60ml coconut cream
- ◆ A handful of ice cubes
- ◆ A slice of pineapple for decoration

## PREPARATION:

1. Take a regular blender and add all the ingredients, except for the decorative pineapple

2. Blitz the mixture until a smooth consistency occurs

3. Take a tall cocktail glass and pour the mixture inside

4. Add the slice of pineapple as decoration

# MINTY MOJITO

*Time 5 minutes, serves 1*
*Net carbs: 4.6g/0.16oz, Fiber: 0g/0oz, Fat: 0.1g/0.003oz,*
*Protein: 0.3g/0.01oz, Kcal: 158*

## INGREDIENTS:

- 60ml white rum

- 1 tsp sugar

- A little soda water, according to your taste

- The juice of 1 lime

- A few fresh mint leaves

- A handful of ice cubes

## PREPARATION:

**1.** Take a small jug and add the sugar, mint leaves (leave a few to one side for decoration), and the lime juice

**2.** Use a muddler to combine, carefully crushing the leaves

**3.** Take a tall cocktail glass and add the muddled mixture into the bottom

**4.** Add a handful of ice cubes on top

5. Carefully pour the rum into the glass

6. Take a long bar spoon and stir carefully to combine the ingredients

7. Add a little soda water on top

8. Decorate with the other mint leaves

# TRADITIONAL MAI TAI

*Time 5 minutes, serves 1*
*Net carbs: 19.6g/0.37oz, Fiber: 0.2g/0.007oz, Fat: 0g/0oz,*
*Protein: 0.1g/0.003oz, Kcal: 284*

## INGREDIENTS:

- 2 tbsp white rum

- 2 tbsp triple sec

- 2 tbsp dark rum

- 1 tbsp almond syrup

- 1 tbsp grenadine

- Half a lime, juiced

- A handful of ice cubs

- 1 maraschino cherry for decoration

## PREPARATION:

| 1. | Take a cocktail shaker and add all the ingredients, apart from the cherry and the ice cubes |

| 2. | Add the ice cubes afterwards and shake until the outside is cold |

| 3. | Pour the cocktail into a tumbler glass |

| 4. | Decorate with the maraschino cherry |

# FROZEN DAIQUIRI

*Time 10 minutes, serves 2*
*Net carbs: 17g/0.59oz, Fiber: 7g/0.24oz, Fat: 1g/0.03oz,*
*Protein: 1g/0.03oz, Kcal: 219*

## INGREDIENTS:

- 100ml rum
- 200g ice
- 500g prepared strawberries
- The juice of half a lime
- 2 lime slices for decoration

## PREPARATION:

1. Take a blender and add the strawberries, to blend down to a fine pulp

2. Once blended, take a small sieve and remove as many seeds from the berries as you can

3. Return the strawberry mixture to the blender and add the lime juice, rum, and the ice

4. Blend until everything is combined and smooth

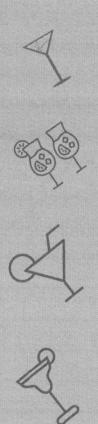

**5.** Take 2 Martini glasses and divide the mixture evenly between the two

**6.** Decorate the glass with lime slices and drink whilst cold

# MOJITO WITH A TWIST

*Time 30 minutes, serves 6*
*Net carbs: 51g/1.79oz, Fiber: 0g/0oz, Fat: 0g/0oz,*
*Protein: 0g/0oz, Kcal: 264*

## INGREDIENTS:

- 150ml rum

- 300g sugar

- 12 mint leaves

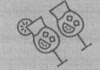

- The juice of 6 limes

- 1 litre of water

- A handful of ice cubes

- 1 juiced bergamot, keep the zest also

## PREPARATION:

| 1. | Take a small saucepan and add the sugar and water |

| 2. | Bring the pan to the boil and remove from the heat, allowing to cool |

| 3. | Take a blender and combine the juice, mint leaves, and the zest from the bergamot |

| 4. | Add the cooled sugar syrup and combine |

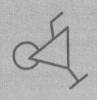

**5.** Take a large plastic jug and pour the mixture inside, placing in the freezer for half an hour

**6.** Take a large cocktail glass and scoop the iced mixture inside

**7.** Pour the rum over the top and enjoy whilst still cold

# ZESTY BERRY PUNCH

*Time 5 minutes, serves 10*
*Net carbs: 17g/0.59oz, Fiber: 0g/0oz, Fat: 0g/0oz,*
*Protein: 0g/0oz, Kcal: 164*

## INGREDIENTS:

- ♦ 350ml rum, dark rum works best with this recipe
- ♦ 1 litre of chilled cranberry juice
- ♦ 1 litre of chilled ginger ale
- ♦ Ice cubes

## PREPARATION:

1. Take a large punch bowl and pour the cranberry juice and ginger ale inside, stirring until combined

2. Pour the rum into the bowl and combine once more

3. Pour into cocktail glasses and top with plenty of ice cubes

# BOOZY COCONUT PUNCH

*Time 5 minutes, serves 4*
*Net carbs: 17g/oz, Fiber: 0g/0.59oz, Fat: 8g/0.28oz,*
*Protein: 1g/0.03oz, Kcal: 241*

## INGREDIENTS:

- ◆ 250ml rum, Malibu is a good choice for this coconut-based cocktail
- ◆ 500ml fresh pineapple juice
- ◆ 500ml fresh mango juice
- ◆ 250ml tinned coconut milk
- ◆ A handful of ice cubes
- ◆ A few slices of pineapple for decoration

## PREPARATION:

| 1. | Take a large mixing jug and add the ingredients together, combing well |
|----|---|
| 2. | Add some ice to each glass |
| 3. | Pour the punch into each glass |
| 4. | Decorate with a slice of pineapple |

# SPICY RUM 75

*Time 20 minutes, serves 5*
*Net carbs: 16g/0.56oz, Fiber: 0g/0oz, Fat: 0g/0oz,*
*Protein: 0g/0oz, Kcal: 207*

## INGREDIENTS:

- 200ml rum

- 600ml champagne, you could use Prosecco if you can't find champagne

- 60g caster sugar

- 30ml water

- 1 tbsp ground allspice

- 90ml fresh lime juice

- A few slices of orange for decoration

## PREPARATION:

| 1. | Take small saucepan and add the sugar, water, and the allspice |

| 2. | Stir gently over a medium heat until the sugar has completely dissolved |

| 3. | Remove the pan from the heat and allow to completely cool |

4.    Once cooled, use a fine sieve to remove any grains of allspice from the mixture

5.    Take a cocktail shaker and add the rum, lime juice, and the strained spice mixture

6.    Combine the mixture by shaking vigorously

7.    Take 6 champagne flutes and divide the mixture evenly between, leaving a little space at the top

8.    Top up the glasses with the champagne or Prosecco

9.    Decorate with a slice of orange

# PINEAPPLE CAIPIRINHAS

*Time 15 minutes, serves 8*
*Net carbs: 80g/2.82oz, Fiber: 2g/0.07oz, Fat: 0g/0oz,*
*Protein: 1g/0.03oz, Kcal: 433*

## INGREDIENTS:

- 400ml light rum. You can also use cachaca liqueur instead
- 800ml fresh pineapple juice
- 1 pineapple, cut into chunks
- A few sprigs of mint
- 8 tbsp caster sugar
- The juice of 4 limes
- Crushed ice

## PREPARATION:

**1.** Take a large pitcher and add around half the pineapple chunks, mint, lime juice, and the sugar

**2.** Use the end of a rolling pin to mash the mixture down into a pulp

**3.** Add the rum or cachaca and combine with the pulp

4. Add the pineapple juice to the top of the pitcher

5. Take 8 glasses and add some crushed ice into each

6. Pour the cocktail into the glasses equally

7. Use any left-over pineapple to decorate the glasses

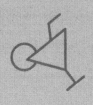

# NON-ALCOHOLIC COCKTAIL RECIPES

Of course, not everyone who attends your home will be an alcohol drinker and in that case you can make delicious cocktails minus the booze to ensure that they don't miss out on the deliciousness! You can also make non-alcoholic cocktails for the teenagers and youngsters at your events too.

The ingredients in non-alcoholic cocktails are generally fruit based, so stock up on ingredients and get creating!

Ironically, non-alcoholic cocktails are also a great way to enjoy delicious drinks when you're trying to keep calories low.

# MOCK MOJITO

*Time 5 minutes, serves 2*
*Net carbs: 9g/oz, Fiber: 0g/0oz, Fat: 0g/0oz,*
*Protein: 0g/0oz, Kcal: 34*

## INGREDIENTS:

- ♦ The juice of 3 limes
- ♦ 1 tbsp caster sugar
- ♦ A small bunch of fresh mint
- ♦ A little soda water to taste
- ♦ Crushed ice

## PREPARATION:

1. Place the mint and sugar in a small bowl and either use the end of a rolling pin to muddle, or use a specialist muddler if you have one already

2. Take 2 tall cocktail glasses and add crushed ice to the bottom of both

3. Pour the sugar mixture into each glass equally and add the lime juice equally too

**4.** Combine the mixtures together

**5.** Add a little soda water to each glass and decorate with a few extra mint leaves

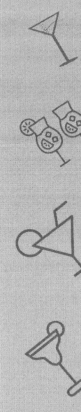

# VIRGIN NEW YORK SOUR

*Time 10 minutes, serves 1*
*Net carbs: 17g/0.59oz, Fiber: 0g/0oz, Fat: 0g/0oz,*
*Protein: 2g/0.07oz, Kcal: 78*

## INGREDIENTS:

- 50ml of strong tea. If you can use assam leaves, these work best

- 25ml fresh lemon juice

- 3 tsp maple syrup

- 10ml fresh pomegranate juice

- 1tbsp egg white

- A little vanilla extract to taste

- A handful of ice cubes

## PREPARATION:

| | |
|---|---|
| 1. | Make up the tea and add the vanilla whilst it's still hot |
| 2. | Place to one side and allow to cool |
| 3. | Take a cocktail shaker and add the maple syrup, lemon juice and the tea |
| 4. | Add the egg white and stir carefully to break up |

**5.** Shake the cocktail shaker. Stop when the mixture is frothy

**6.** Add a handful of ice cubes to the shaker and combine once more, until the outside of the shaker is cold

**7.** Fill up a cocktail glass with a little more ice

**8.** Strain the mixture into the cocktail glass

**9.** Take a small measuring jug and add the pomegranate juice, adding water until it reaches the 20ml mark

**10.** Pour the pomegranate into the glass slowly - the foam will remain on top

# FALSE NEGRONI

*Time 20 minutes, serves 1*
*Net carbs: 15g/0.52oz, Fiber: 0g/0oz, Fat: 0g/0oz,*
*Protein: 0g/0oz, Kcal: 61*

## INGREDIENTS:

- Half a grapefruit

- 125g caster sugar

- 125ml water

- 25ml cold water

- 1 slice of fresh orange

- A few coriander seeds

- 3 crushed cardamom pods

- 25ml grape juice, white grape juice is best for this cocktail

- A handful of ice cubes

## PREPARATION:

1. Take the grapefruit and peel carefully. Cut the fruit into chunks

2. Take a medium saucepan and add the grapefruit, sugar, slice of orange, cardamom pods, coriander seeds, and the 125ml of water

3. Heat over a medium heat until the mixture begins to simmer. Once that's happens stir on a simmer for 5 minutes, making sure that you keep pushing the fruit down with the back of your spoon so it turns into a pulp

4. Remove the pan from the heat once the fruit is completely soft and mushy

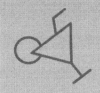

5. Allow to cool

6. Once the contents of the pan are cool, take a bowl and strain the mixture thoroughly. You can throw away any of the seeds or pieces left over

7. Take a tumbler and add some ice

8. Add 25ml of the strained syrup to the glass, along with the grape juice and 25ml of cold water

**9.** Stir the contents of the glass carefully

**10.** Serve when the outside of the glass feels cold

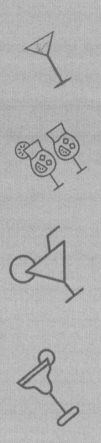

# PEACH LONG ISLAND ICE TEA

*Time 15 minutes, serves 12*
*Net carbs: 19g/0.67oz, Fiber: 1g/0.03oz, Fat: 0g/0oz,*
*Protein: 0.3g/0.01oz, Kcal: 78*

## INGREDIENTS:

- 4 peaches with stones removed, chopped into pieces

- 1 sliced peach for decoration

- 200g sugar

- 250ml water

- 2 litres of boiling water

- 4 regular teabags

- Plenty of ice cues

## PREPARATION:

| 1. | Take a medium pan and add the sugar and 150ml water |

| 2. | Heat and bring to the boil, stirring until the sugar has completely dissolved |

| 3. | Add the peach pieces and continue to stir, cooking until the peach has gone soft |

4. Remove the pan from the heat and mash the peach with the back of a fork

5. Place to one side for an hour

6. Once ready, run the syrup through a sieve to remove any small pieces and scared any chunks

7. Mash the mixture down until it is very pulpy

8. Take a large glass mixing jug and add the teabags, pouring 2 litres of boing water over the top

9. Place to one side for 4 minutes, stir and remove the tea bags, discharging them.

10. Allow the tea to cool and then place in the refrigerator to chill

11. Once read to serve, take a tall glass and pour half of the peach syrup inside, topping up with the iced tea

12. Add some ice cubes, or if you prefer, you could add a little sparkling water too

13. Decorate with peach slices

# G&T WITHOUT THE GIN!

*Time 10 minutes, serves 6*
*Net carbs: 5g/0.17oz, Fiber: 0g/0oz, Fat: 0g/0oz,*
*Protein: 0.2g/0.007oz, Kcal: 21*

## INGREDIENTS:

- Half a fresh cucumber

- The zest of 1 lemon

- 5 cloves

- 5 cardamom pods

- 1 teabag, chamomile works best

- A small bunch of fresh mint leaves

- Half a bunch of fresh rosemary

- Tonic water to taste

- 500ml cold water

- A handful of ice cubes

## PREPARATION:

| 1. | Take the cardamom pods and crush to bruise |

| 2. | Slice up the cucumber thinly |

3. Take a large jug and add both the cucumber and cardamom pods inside

4. Add the teabag, lemon zest, rosemary, mint, and the cloves

5. Add 500ml of cold water and stir well

6. Place in the refrigerator for at least 2 hours

7. When you're ready to serve, take a glass and add 50ml of the mixture inside

8. Pour enough tonic water on top to take the mixture to the top of the glass

9. Add a few ice cubes and garnish with a little extra mint

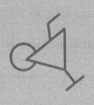

# TROPICAL PUNCH MOCKTAIL

*Time 10 minutes, serves 8*
*Net carbs: 5g/0.17oz, Fiber: 0g/0oz, Fat: 0g/0oz,*
*Protein: 0g/0oz, Kcal: 52*

## INGREDIENTS:

- ◆ 1 peeled kiwi fruit, chopped into pieces

- ◆ 2 fresh rings of pineapple, chopped into pieces

- ◆ A few strawberries, cut into halves

- ◆ Soda water to taste

- ◆ Sparkling apple juice to taste

- ◆ Fruit juice to taste, the tropical version of this works best and gives extra flavour to the punch

- ◆ A handful of ice cubes

## PREPARATION:

1. Take a large mixing bowl and add the kiwi fruit, pineapple pieces, and the strawberries, combining everything together well

2. Take 8 large glasses and add a little of the fruit mixture to the bottom of each one

**3.** Top up the glasses with equal measurements of the tropical juice, apple juice and a little soda water

**4.** Add a few ice cubes and serve

# POMEGRANATE NOT-MOJITO

*Time 10 minutes, serves 8*
*Net carbs: 18g/0.63oz, Fiber: 0g/0oz, Fat: 0g/0oz,*
*Protein: 1g/0.03oz, Kcal: 76*

## INGREDIENTS:

- ◆ 2 limes but into quarters

- ◆ A few lime slices for decoration

- ◆ 1 litre of fresh pomegranate juice

- ◆ A large bunch of fresh mint

- ◆ 3 tbsp pomegranate seeds

- ◆ 500ml cold lemonade

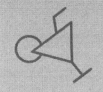

## PREPARATION:

| 1. | Place the pomegranate seeds into an empty ice cube tray and top up with water. Place in the freezer until completely frozen |

| 2. | Take half of the mint leaves and place into a large jug, adding the quarters of lime |

| 3. | Take a rolling pin and crush the contents of the bowl until the juices and flavours are completely released |

4. Add the lemonade and the pomegranate juice to the bowl and combine

5. Take large cocktail glasses and add a couple of pomegranate ice cubes into the bottom of each glass

6. Strain the cocktail mixture into each glass evenly

7. Decorate with lime slices and the rest of the mint remaining

# BERRY MOCKTAIL

*Time 15 minutes, serves 1*
*Net carbs: 7g/0.24oz, Fiber: 0g/0oz, Fat: 0g/0oz,*
*Protein: 0g/0oz, Kcal: 28*

## INGREDIENTS:

- ◆ 1 sprig of fresh mint, chopped

- ◆ 120ml sparkling lemonade

- ◆ 1 fresh cucumber, cut into small pieces

- ◆ A handful of red berries, either fresh or frozen

- ◆ 200ml water

- ◆ A handful of ice cubes

- ◆ A few slices of orange and lime for decoration

## PREPARATION:

| 1. | Take a small pan and add the mint and cucumber pieces |
|---|---|
| 2. | Add 200ml of water and bring to the boil |
| 3. | Stir until combined and remove from the heat |
| 4. | Add the berries and allow to soften, before using the back a fork to crush and squash everything down |

**5.** Once cooled completely, strain the mixture into a bowl

**6.** Take a tall glass and add 40ml of the mixture

**7.** Add a few ice cubes and add the lemonade to the top of the glass, stirring gently

**8.** Decorate with orange and lime slices

# RHUBARB SUMMER MOCKTAIL

*Time 20 minutes, serves 10*
*Net carbs: 12g/0.42oz, Fiber: 0.1g/0.03oz, Fat: 0g/0oz,*
*Protein: 0g/0oz, Kcal: 49*

## INGREDIENTS:

- The juice and zest of 1 orange
- The juice and zest of 1 lemon
- 300g caster sugar
- 450g fresh, chopped rhubarb
- 300ml water
- 1 peeled slice of root ginger, fresh
- Sparkling water to taste
- A handful of ice cubes

## PREPARATION:

1. Take a large pan and add the water and sugar

2. Allow the mixture to reach a simmer and stir until the sugar is dissolved

3. Add the orange zest and juice, then the lemon zest juice, and stir

4. Add the ginger and the rhubarb and combine once more

5. Cook on a low-medium heat and stir regularly until the rhubarb starts to soften and tear apart

6. Remove the pan from the heat and pour the mixture through a sieve into a heatproof measuring jug

7. Transfer the mixture into sterilised jars. This mixture can be stored in the refrigerator for up to 4 weeks

8. When you're ready to serve, take a cocktail glass and add a handful of ice to the bottom

9. Pour 25ml of the rhubarb mixture into the glass and add sparkling water according to your personal taste

# MULLED WINE, WITHOUT THE WINE

*Time 20 minutes, serves 6*
*Net carbs: 19g/0.67oz, Fiber: 1g/0.03oz, Fat: 0g/0oz,*
*Protein: 0.5g/0.01oz, Kcal: 83*

## INGREDIENTS:

- 25g caster sugar
- 250ml fresh apple juice
- 500ml fresh pomegranate juice
- 4 cloves
- 1 orange, cut into quarters
- A few blackberries, either fresh or frozen
- 1 stick of cinnamon
- 3 black peppercorns
- 1 star anise
- A few slices of orange for decoration

## PREPARATION:

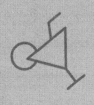

**1.** Take a large saucepan and add the fresh pomegranate juice, the blackberries, the app juice, and the sugar, combining everything carefully

**2.** Next, add the cloves, cinnamon stick, star anise, orange quarter and the peppercorns, stirring again

**3.** Heat over a low setting until the mixture begins to simmer, stirring regularly

**4.** Carefully test the mixture (be careful, it's hot!) to see how it tastes. If you need it sweeter, add a little more sugar

**5.** Once ready, remove the pan from the heat and strain into a heatproof glass

**6.** Decorate with a few orange slices

# CONCLUSION

You now have all the knowledge and information you need to create delicious cocktails in the comfort of your own home. As you can see from the recipes we've talked about throughout this book, most ingredients are very easy to find and you can focus on the type of spirit you prefer when mixing your favourite drinks. If you prefer to go down the non-alcoholic route, there is plenty of choice there too.

Cocktail making is one of the most in-demand hobbies. The ability to create delicious and impressive cocktails for your guests is something not everyone can claim to do, so if you can master the basic skills and practice until you're perfect, you'll certainly gain a reputation as quite the host or hostess when you have dinner parties or other events in your home!

Of course, not everyone wants to go out to expensive bars at the weekend either. In that case, you don't have to miss out on delicious cocktails and relaxation, you simply whip up a batch beforehand, place them in the refrigerator, and enjoy from the comfort of your own home, garden, or anywhere else you choose.

All that's left to do now is to practice your new skills, choose your first recipe, and get started. In no time at all, you'll be shaking those cocktails like Tom Cruise in Cocktail!

# DISCLAIMER

This book contains opinions and ideas of the author and is meant to teach the reader informative and helpful knowledge while due care should be taken by the user in the application of the information provided. The instructions and strategies are possibly not right for every reader and there is no guarantee that they work for everyone. Using this book and implementing the information/recipes therein contained is explicitly your own responsibility and risk. This work with all its contents, does not guarantee correctness, completion, quality or correctness of the provided information. Misinformation or misprints cannot be completely eliminated.

Printed in Great Britain
by Amazon

19595884R00064